From The
PULPIT
To The
PEW

7 Steps to Elevate Your Church Leadership

John K. Lomax

Copyright © [2025] John K. Lomax

Dedication

To my dearly departed mother, **Willie Mae Lomax**, the real gem in my spiritual life, whose unwavering faith and guidance set me on the path to serve God with all my heart.

To the late **William E. Diggs**, my spiritual leader for over 30 years, who exemplified grace, wisdom, and steadfast devotion to the Lord.

And to my dear wife of 32 years, **Dorothy**, the love of my life, who has been my constant companion, my wisest counselor, and my greatest earthly blessing.

Testimonials

This book serves as a transformative roadmap to empower your journey toward unlocking your ultimate potential, not only as a leader but, more profoundly, as a radiant ambassador of Jesus Christ. This book is anchored in profound doctrine, overflowing with practical wisdom and timeless relevance.

Rev. Devin D. Paylor

In a world where effective leadership is crucial, **From the Pulpit to the Pew: 7 Steps to Elevate Your Church Leadership** stands out as a beacon for church leaders seeking to inspire and guide their congregations. This book brilliantly bridges the gap between spiritual guidance and practical leadership strategies, offering an insightful and actionable step-by-step approach. Written with compassion and wisdom, it provides a roadmap for elevating your leadership skills and ensuring that your influence resonates from the pulpit and throughout your entire Church and community. Whether you are a seasoned leader or just beginning your journey, this book is an invaluable resource that will empower you to lead with purpose and conviction.

Rev. Dr. Debora Lawson Smith

Persimmon Grove AME Church

This book is awesome…as a new Pastor these are invaluable nuggets that I can use to make me a better leader…your leadership points are good for all aspects of life and you always bring it back to the basic principles of our faith. I think I will purchase copies as gifts for some of my colleagues.

Reverend LaTanya Pender

I found this book very inspiring. You spoke much truth in this powerful little book. I liked the way that you not only talked about Scripture but you used Scripture effectively all throughout the book. This work has so much potential to help people grow. I liked this book so much that I will give copies to my daughter and my son. I highly recommend it to all who are in leadership and to all who want to serve.
Dr.Conrad K. Pridgen,
Retired Presiding Elder
Western North Carolina Conference
The Second District AME Church

All glory to God! As one who led a business John served early in his professional career, I'm thrilled to see this much needed synthesis of what he has learned along the way in his experiences as a Bible-centered follower of Christ, church leader, and able business executive. Having read scores of books on Christian servant leadership for both church and business settings, I see John's contribution as refreshingly practical, well-organized, and useful for those at any level seeking to enhance their walk with our Lord while better serving those God has entrusted to their care. Brother Lomax's call to lead a faithful, integrated life in Christ – characterized by Christlike humility and love, and lifelong learning and accountability – will help its readers to build trust and serve others well as they "press on" and finish the race strong for Christ with eternity in mind!

Don Barefoot

Principal, IntegrityCEOAdvisors.com

Former CEO of The C12 Group, America's leading Christian CEO equipping organization

Table of Contents

Introduction 1

Chapter 1 Scripture, Prayer, and Meditation, —Laying the Foundation of Effective Leadership 4

    Reflection Questions 22

Chapter 2 Never Stop Learning—Cultivating a Lifelong Appetite for Growth 24

    Reflection Questions 45

Chapter 3 Seek Wisdom and Discernment—Choosing the Road Less Traveled 46

    Reflection Questions 61

Chapter 4 Find Your Blind Spots—Seeing What You Can't See .. 62

    Reflection Questions 79

Chapter 5 Find Your Passion and What You're Really Good At—Aligning Your Gifts with God's Calling 80

    Reflection Questions 96

Chapter 6 Stretch Beyond Where You Are—Breaking Through Fear and Doubt 97

    Reflection Questions 111

Chapter 7 Learn to Walk in Love—The Greatest Commandment for Leadership 112

    Reflection Questions 128

Conclusion Transforming Leadership Through Faith, Wisdom, and Love 129

Acknowledgments 143

About the Author 144

A Personal Note from John K. Lomax

Thank you so much for choosing to purchase this book directly from my website. Your support truly means the world to me! It's my heartfelt prayer that **From The Pulpit To The** Pew becomes a source of inspiration and guidance in your leadership journey, faith exploration, and everyday choices.

I've dedicated years of ministry, business experience, and personal development to what you'll find within these pages. It's a privilege to accompany you on your path as you discover and embrace your purpose and power.

Keep your spirits high, and let's stay connected!

Warm wishes,

John K. Lomax

https://johnklomax.com/

Introduction

Leadership is not just a role, it's a calling. Whether in the church, the workplace, or the community, the call to lead is both a privilege and a responsibility. My name is **John K. Lomax**, and over the course of my life, I have been blessed to serve in leadership roles that have shaped me, stretched me, and drawn me closer to God. From my time as a Sunday School Superintendent, Bible teacher, and Director of Christian Education, to my years as a C-suite executive in the corporate world, I've learned that the principles of godly leadership are timeless, transformative, and deeply rooted in love.

I didn't always understand this. In 1991, I was convicted of death by motor vehicle and sentenced to five years in prison. That season of brokenness could have defined my life, but by

God's grace, it became the foundation for my redemption. Over the next three decades, God opened doors I never could have imagined, leading me from that low point to retiring in 2023 as the Chief Operations Officer (COO) of a multi-million-dollar corporation. Through it all, the church has been my sanctuary and my guide, shaping me into the man I am today.

In this book, I want to share seven **key principles** that have transformed my life and leadership. These principles are not just about becoming a more effective leader—they're about becoming the leader God has called you to be, a true servant leader and ambassador for Christ. Whether you're a pastor, a lay leader, or someone seeking to grow in your faith, my hope is that this book will inspire you to lead with faith, wisdom, and love. Together, let's explore how these principles can elevate your leadership, strengthen your walk with

God, and empower you to make a lasting impact for His Kingdom.

Chapter 1
Scripture, Prayer, and Meditation, — Laying the Foundation of Effective Leadership

There is no more critical starting point in a journey of Christian leadership than Scripture study, prayer, and meditation. These three spiritual disciplines anchor us in a reality greater than our own ideas, ambitions, or emotions. When we engage in daily, intentional communication with God, we cultivate hearts that are attuned to His voice and wills that are submitted to His purposes. For any leader—be it a pastor, teacher, volunteer coordinator, or lay minister—this foundation is indispensable. Without it, our leadership lacks the spiritual grounding that ensures our ministry is powered by the Holy Spirit rather than human effort alone. When we devote ourselves to prayer, quiet contemplation, and the study of God's Word, we align our hearts with the One who called us in the first place.

The study of God's Word must come first. The Bible is not just another book; it is the inspired Word of God, declaring His will and revealing the path of salvation through Jesus Christ, His Son. While other faith traditions emphasize study, prayer, and meditation, what sets Christian leadership apart is our foundation—the Bible as the ultimate authority. The Bible alone declares Jesus as the Son of God, the Savior of the world, and the way, the truth, and the life (John 14:6). So, all Christian leaders should start by studying the Word of God and letting it be our guiding force. Once we open our hearts and minds to God's Word, we then need to pray for guidance, and finally, we need to meditate on the Word and the things that God has placed in front of us to lead so that we can move forward with clarity, wisdom, discernment, grace, mercy and above all with love.

However, many people struggle to integrate these practices into their daily lives. Modern schedules are often packed with meetings, family responsibilities, commuting, and an onslaught of digital notifications. Some might say, "I just can't find the time," but I've learned that we make time for what we value most. If we truly believe that prayer, meditation, and Scripture reading are the bedrocks of effective Christian living and leadership, we will carve out the space necessary to commune with God. It's less about having enough hours in the day and more about having enough desire in our hearts. For me, these moments of connection take on many forms. Sometimes if I have only a few moments to commune with my Savior I may sing a simple song of praise and thanksgiving. I've found that combining Scripture, prayer, and praise into a simple act of worship allows me to commune with God, even on the busiest days. This practice became a lifeline during my time at Sandy Ridge Prison, where two men from a Methodist church in Jamestown, NC, would come and sing gospel songs on Sunday mornings. They introduced me to songs rooted in Scripture, such as Psalm 25:1-2 and Psalm 48:1-2, which have remained a part of my daily meditation for over 30 years. Every morning, I rise and sing—sometimes softly to myself, sometimes aloud, and occasionally with my wife joining me.

One of my favorites is Psalm 25:1-2:

"Unto Thee, O Lord, do I lift up my soul.
O my God, I trust in Thee, let me not be ashamed,
let not my enemies triumph over me."

I often sing the verses over and over until I feel the presence of the Lord. In these few brief moments, I've spoken Scripture, prayed, and meditated on His Word through a simple melody.

Another favorite is Psalm 48:1-2:

"Great is the Lord and greatly to be praised In the city of our God, in the mountain of His holiness. Beautiful situation, the joy of the whole earth, is Mount Zion on the sides of the north, The city of the great King."

These songs have carried me through decades, reminding me of God's presence and power in every season of life. Whether I have hours or just moments to spare, these simple acts of worship keep me anchored. My connection to God doesn't always require elaborate rituals—it's often found in a heartfelt song, a whispered prayer, or a moment of stillness filled with His Word. God stands ready to meet us when we approach Him in faith, whether that's for fifteen minutes on a busy weekday morning or an extended hour before dawn.

Prayer and meditation are essential, but they must flow from our engagement with Scripture. The study of God's Word grounds us in truth, equips us to discern His voice, and strengthens us to lead His people with wisdom and integrity. Without a deep understanding of Scripture, our prayer and meditation lack the anchor of divine truth. Our study is not simply an intellectual exercise but a spiritual discipline that transforms our hearts and minds (Romans 12:2). When we pray, we communicate with God, and when we meditate, we reflect on His Word and listen for His guidance. However, without the foundation of the Bible, our prayers risk becoming self-centered, and our meditation may wander into the realm of human reasoning. Psalm 1 reminds us of the blessedness of meditating on God's law day and night, promising that such a person will be like a tree planted by streams of water, bearing fruit in every season.

It is important to emphasize that effective church leadership is not about charisma, programs, or personal ambition. It is about submission to

God's authority, as revealed in His Word. Leaders must be diligent in studying the Bible, not just for sermons or lessons, but to know God personally and intimately. As Paul instructed Timothy, "Study to show yourself approved unto God, a worker who does not need to be ashamed, rightly dividing the word of truth" (2 Timothy 2:15).

This is the foundation: Study first. Pray fervently. Meditate deeply. When these disciplines are in balance, they empower us to lead with humility, clarity, and a God-centered vision. Jesus modeled this for us. Though He often withdrew to pray, His words and actions were always grounded in the Scriptures. As leaders, we must follow His example.

In the chapters that follow, we will explore how these foundational disciplines integrate with the practical challenges of church leadership. But it all begins here: with a firm commitment to the study of God's Word. For only through His Word can we fully know His will, live in His power, and lead His people faithfully.

There is a well-known president at a famous local university who rises each day at 4:30 or 5:00 a.m. so he can walk and meditate in prayer before his schedule fills up. That story sticks with me, because it underscores the fact that even people with demanding professions—even those who might work in highly intellectual, secular environments—understand the transformative power of a few daily quiet moments with God. For years, I have followed my own routine of rising early to give my first moments to the Lord. I typically wake up at 5:00 a.m. My wife, who is able to sleep in a bit longer, usually doesn't rise until 6:30, which grants me a precious hour and a half of solitude. During at least thirty of those minutes, I dedicate myself to Studying his Word, meditating on God's Word, speaking to Him in prayer, and listening for His gentle guidance in the stillness.

Many people struggle to integrate these practices into their daily lives… Some might say, "I just can't find the time," but I've learned that we make time for what we value most. If we truly believe that prayer, meditation, and Scripture reading are the bedrocks of effective Christian living and leadership, we will carve out the space necessary to commune with God.

Why are prayer, meditation, and Scripture so tightly woven? Prayer is our direct conversation with God—our opportunity to share our fears, hopes, and praises, while also seeking direction and divine wisdom. Meditation, meanwhile, is the practice of quieting the noise in our minds to reflect deeply on God's truths, character, and promises. Rather than emptying our minds (as some secular forms of meditation suggest), we fill them with the reality of God's presence and the richness of His Word. Scripture, of course, is the living and active Word of God (Hebrews 4:12). When we study it, we're not merely reading ancient text; we're engaging with God's timeless revelation, discovering who He is, what He has done, and how He calls us to live.

In leadership, we often face complex challenges: difficult decision-making, interpersonal conflicts, organizational stress, or even personal doubts about our calling. It's easy to let anxiety or ambition drive us rather than God's wisdom. Prayer keeps us tethered to the Source of true guidance, reminding us that we are servants first and foremost. When we pray, we acknowledge our human limitations and invite the Holy Spirit to lead us. Meditation then allows us to truly digest what God is saying—either through the Scriptures we've read or the impressions He's placed on our hearts. It becomes a sacred pause, where the chaos of life recedes and the voice of God takes center stage. And Scripture grounds everything in unchanging truth, preventing us from relying solely on emotions or personal biases. In a sense, these three disciplines form a cycle: Scripture informs our prayers, prayer ignites our meditation, and meditation brings the Word to life in our hearts.

In leadership, we often face complex challenges: difficult decision-making, interpersonal conflicts, organizational stress, or even personal doubts about our calling… prayer keeps us tethered to the Source of true guidance!

One powerful exercise is to take a single verse from your daily Bible reading and carry it with you throughout the day. Write it on a notecard or store it in your phone. Periodically pause to reread and reflect on that verse. Ask the Holy Spirit to show you how to apply it. For instance, if your verse for the day is Philippians 4:6— "Do not be anxious about anything, but in everything by prayer and supplication with thanksgiving let your requests be made known to God"—you might pause whenever you sense worry creeping in. Take a short prayer break, offering your concerns to God, and thank Him for His faithfulness. In doing so, you're practicing prayer, meditation, and Scripture engagement all at once. Over time, this habit can dramatically shift your mindset and behavior, embedding God's truth in the minutes of daily life.

It's important to note that these spiritual practices aren't reserved for early birds or those with flexible schedules. You can carve out fifteen minutes anytime, anywhere. Some people use their lunch breaks to quietly read a Psalm or practice breath prayers—short, simple prayers repeated in tune with their breathing. Others find a brief window in the evening, after the day's demands have settled, to quietly process everything with God. If you're in a season of life where personal space is scarce—perhaps you have small children or multiple jobs—be creative. Maybe it's ten minutes in the car before heading into work, or fifteen minutes after the kids go to bed. The real key is consistency. When we consistently meet with God, even in small increments, we train our spirits to recognize His presence throughout the day.

For leaders, this consistency is not a luxury; it's a necessity. We are spiritual shepherds, whether we oversee a church, a ministry team, or simply our own household. Those under our care need leaders who are in sync with the heartbeat of God. They benefit from our gentleness, our discernment, and our reliance on the Holy Spirit. Each day spent in prayer, meditation, and Scripture refines these qualities within us. It's the difference between leading from a place of anxiety and inadequacy versus leading from a place of peace and conviction. And as we grow in our communion with God, we'll also find ourselves better equipped to deal with inevitable challenges.

Let me challenge you right now: commit to finding at least fifteen minutes a day for these spiritual disciplines. Mark it on your calendar like any other appointment—because it's that important. Imagine how transformative it could be if, every day, you paused to immerse yourself in God's presence before tackling your to-do list. Picture how your mindset might shift if, every night, you ended the day by meditating on a biblical promise rather than scrolling through social media. This isn't about legalism or checking a box. It's about an invitation to deepen your relationship with the Creator, letting

His Word shape your perspectives and His Spirit guide your decisions.

In my own life, I've seen how these practices have grounded me through trials, successes, and everything in between. When I was an inmate, prayer became my lifeline to hope. I recognized that I had reached the end of my own ability to control my situation, and all I could do was lean on a God who promised never to leave me nor forsake me. Meditation and Scripture study illuminated my heart to the possibility that even my worst moments could be used for God's glory. Later, as a busy COO and church leader, these same disciplines provided moments of clarity in the midst of hectic schedules and high-stakes decisions. They reminded me that every ounce of leadership influence I held was a stewardship from God, to be directed by His wisdom, not my ego.

Wherever you find yourself today—whether you're shepherding a large congregation, volunteering on a ministry team, or simply seeking growth in personal devotion—know that prayer, meditation, and Scripture study are foundational. They prepare our hearts for every other aspect of leadership we'll explore in this guide. Start small if you must. Be patient with yourself, but also be diligent. Over time, these disciplines will shape your character, deepen your faith, and infuse your leadership with supernatural grace. So, take that first step: find a quiet corner, open your heart, and let God speak. He's waiting to transform not just your day, but your entire life and leadership journey.

Reflections Chapter 1: Scripture, Prayer, and Meditation—Laying the Foundation of Effective Leadership

Trustworthy Servant leadership begins with a strong spiritual foundation. Prayer aligns our hearts with God's will, meditation creates space to hear His voice, and Scripture provides the unchanging truth that guides our decisions. These three disciplines are inseparable and essential for anyone seeking to lead effectively.

Reflection Questions:

1. How can you create consistent time for prayer, meditation, and Scripture in your daily routine?

2. What specific Scripture passages inspire or guide your leadership?

3. Who in your life can hold you accountable for maintaining a strong spiritual foundation and exercising godly influence even under the most difficult circumstances?

Wherever you find yourself today—whether you're shepherding a large congregation, volunteering on a ministry team, or simply seeking growth in personal devotion—know that prayer, meditation, and Scripture study are foundational.

Chapter 2
Never Stop Learning—Cultivating a Lifelong Appetite for Growth

One of the greatest pitfalls any leader can face is the illusion that they have "arrived." The moment we arrogantly start believing we have learned all there is to learn, or that we can operate effectively on autopilot we begin a slow descent into mediocrity. True leadership—whether in the church, a nonprofit, or a Fortune 500 company—demands a commitment to continuous improvement in serving others. It requires that we maintain a posture of discovery, always seeking to grow intellectually, spiritually, and emotionally. This chapter explores why being a perpetual student is essential for effective leadership, drawing from both real-world business experiences and the practical realities of church service.

Embracing a Learning Mindset

If leadership is influence, then learning is the fuel that propels that influence forward. Leaders who refuse to learn ultimately sabotage their own effectiveness and stifle the potential of those they lead. Many of us, especially within the church, are tempted to think that once we've completed a round of theological training or attended enough leadership conferences, we've reached a plateau of competence. Yet nothing could be further from the truth. **Proverbs 1:5** reminds us, "Let the wise hear and increase in learning, and the one who understands obtain guidance." Scripture itself testifies that wisdom grows with continued exposure to new insights, experiences, and viewpoints.

When I was working in the corporate world, serving in a small C-suite team for a multi-million-dollar corporation, the CEO and president enforced a quarterly reading requirement. Each quarter, our tight-knit leadership group would select a new business or leadership book to read, analyze, and discuss. Often, we'd draw out strategies or principles that we believed could improve our company's operation—whether it was in marketing, organizational structure, or team culture. At first, it felt like yet another task on top of our already daunting to-do lists. But as we consistently engaged with new material, we found ourselves energized by fresh ideas. We discovered strategies that not only refined our business practices but also sharpened our relationships with each other as leaders. The discussions pushed us to question our assumptions, reevaluate our processes, and remain open to innovative solutions. This exercise in continuous learning had another benefit: it kept our leadership humble.

*True leadership —
whether in the church, a
nonprofit, or a Fortune
500 company —
demands a commitment to
continuous improvement
in serving others.*

Proverbs 1:5 reminds us, "Let the wise hear and increase in learning, and the one who understands obtain guidance."

When you're reading a book by someone like Jim Collins—whose research in Good to Great reveals why some organizations soar while others stall—you're forced to confront your own blind spots. You realize that no matter what your title, you still have room to grow and plenty of mistakes to avoid. Over time, our team came to anticipate these quarterly check-ins, seeing them as an opportunity to stretch ourselves beyond the familiar.

Learning Through Collaboration: Visiting, Observing, and Sharing

Beyond books, some of the best learning opportunities come through **collaborating with other leaders**. As church leaders, we can often become isolated in our own ministries, focusing so intensely on our challenges that we miss opportunities to learn from others. Christian leadership thrives when it is practiced within a community of like-minded believers. The journey of leadership is not meant to be walked alone; instead, it is enriched and sharpened through relationships that hold us accountable, encourage our growth, and spur us on toward love and good deeds. As Proverbs 27:17 reminds us, "Iron sharpens iron, and one man sharpens another."

The Power of Like-Minded Community

In Hebrews 10:23-25, we are exhorted to "hold fast the confession of our hope without wavering, for He who promised is faithful. And let us consider how to stir up one another to love and good works, not neglecting to meet together, as is the habit of some, but encouraging one another." These verses underscore the importance of coming together with other believers to grow in faith and to fulfill God's purposes for our lives. A like-minded community provides a Christ-centered environment where trust, safety, and encouragement can flourish. It is within these spaces that leaders can be vulnerable about their challenges, receive wise counsel, and experience the sharpening of their skills and character. In this collaborative setting, the focus is not on competition but on collective growth, as each member contributes to the other's development.

For such communities to be truly effective, a safe, Christ-centered environment is essential for honest conversations and meaningful interactions. Leaders of these groups must establish clear goals and boundaries that prioritize spiritual growth, mutual respect, and adherence to biblical principles. Leaders should ensure everyone's voice is heard and valued. In such settings, members are encouraged to ask hard questions, challenge each other's assumptions, and offer constructive feedback—all while remaining rooted in love and humility. This mirrors Paul's admonition in

Ephesians 4:15 to "speak the truth in love" so that we may grow in every way into Christ, who is the head of the body.

Iron Sharpens Iron

The imagery of "iron sharpening iron" is a vivid reminder that growth often requires friction. Just as a blade becomes sharper through contact with another piece of iron, so too do leaders become more effective when they engage with others who challenge and refine them. This process, while sometimes uncomfortable, is invaluable in shaping leaders who are resilient, wise, and effective in their calling.

In practical terms, this might involve:

1. **Regular Peer Group Meetings:** Gathering with a small group of fellow leaders to

discuss challenges, share insights, and pray for one another.
2. **Mentorship Relationships:** Seeking out mentors who can offer wisdom and guidance while also mentoring others in turn.
3. **Structured Learning Opportunities:** Participating in workshops, retreats, or study groups designed to equip leaders with tools for spiritual and practical growth.

The Outcome of Collaboration

When leaders commit to learning in a community, they model humility and openness, qualities that inspire those they lead. They also gain a broader perspective, as the collective wisdom of the group often surpasses individual understanding. This collaborative approach not only strengthens the individual leader but also builds up the entire body of Christ. In the context of church leadership, this means healthier congregations, more effective ministry, and a greater witness to the world. As Jesus Himself said, "By this all people will know that you are my disciples, if you have love for one another" (John 13:35). By leaning into the power of accountable peer relationships and fostering a Christ-centered community, leaders can grow in their faith, refine their skills, and fulfill their God-given purpose with excellence and integrity.

Visiting other churches with thriving programs in areas where you may be struggling can provide invaluable insights. For example, if your youth ministry is struggling, consider spending a Sunday or even a week shadowing a church with a vibrant youth program. Observe how they engage their teens, structure their events, and build relationships. If you're launching a new outreach initiative but feel stuck, reach out to leaders who've already been successful in similar projects. Not only will you gain practical ideas, but you'll also build relationships with peers who can offer ongoing advice and encouragement.

Attending seminars and conferences is another critical avenue for growth. These events expose you to innovative ideas, cutting-edge tools, and powerful teaching from seasoned leaders. Conferences often provide an environment of inspiration and connection, where you can meet other leaders who are facing similar challenges and exchange strategies. Make it a point to attend at least one conference a year, whether it's a church leadership summit, a denominational gathering, or a specialized workshop on a topic like discipleship, church planting, or financial management. The investment of time and resources will pay dividends as you return home refreshed and equipped to lead with renewed clarity.

The Role of Mentorship

No matter how seasoned you are as a leader, having a mentor is invaluable. A mentor brings wisdom, perspective, and guidance (including encouragement and life-on-life accountability before the Lord) that can sharpen your skills and help you navigate challenges. In my own journey, mentors have been instrumental in helping me recognize areas for growth, stay accountable to my goals, and remain encouraged when the road feels tough.

When seeking a mentor, look for someone who demonstrates both spiritual maturity and leadership competence. This doesn't necessarily have to be someone from your immediate context. In fact, sometimes the best mentors are those who lead in a different sphere or organization, as they can provide a fresh perspective. A mentor can help you see what's possible when you're stuck and gently correct you when you veer off course.

If you're already established as a leader, consider also **becoming a mentor** to others. Mentoring creates a two-way learning dynamic: as you pour into someone else's life, you often find yourself learning just as much from their questions, struggles, and insights. It's a practical way to multiply leadership capacity within the Kingdom while staying in a mindset of growth. In addition, as leaders, we are called not only to guide those around us but also to prepare the next generation of leaders. Jesus' Great Commission commands us to "make disciples of all nations… teaching them to observe all that I have commanded you" (Matthew 28:19-20). This call to disciple-making is not limited to evangelism; it extends to mentorship—walking alongside others to nurture their growth in faith and leadership. Paul's words in 2 Timothy 2:2 further emphasize this responsibility: "And what you have heard from me in the presence of many witnesses entrust to faithful men, who will be able to teach others also." Effective mentorship involves equipping others with the tools and wisdom they need to lead well, ensuring that the work of the Kingdom continues to thrive beyond our own lifetimes. In this way, mentorship becomes a vital extension of collaboration, as experienced leaders invest in the spiritual and practical development of emerging leaders.

Continual Study in Ministry

In my current role as a Church School Superintendent and bible teacher, I've seen firsthand how the demand to teach others forces you to become a perpetual student. Every week as a bible teacher, you are preparing lessons, reviewing Scripture, and fielding questions from individuals with unique perspectives. Their curiosities challenge you to go deeper into biblical context, theology, and application. Teaching isn't merely disseminating facts; it's an ongoing dialogue that enriches you as much as it enlightens those you serve.

This active engagement with learning isn't just beneficial—it's transformative. The more I study to instruct others, the more I realize how vast and beautiful Scripture truly is. I also see how essential it is to bring in insights from a broad range of sources—biblical commentaries, historical studies, and sometimes even business or leadership frameworks. Jesus Himself often used illustrations from everyday life—agriculture, finances, relationships—to communicate profound spiritual truths. Why shouldn't we, as modern church leaders, be similarly well-rounded in our learning?

Overcoming Barriers to Continuous Learning

Many leaders resist the call to "never stop learning" because they feel overloaded. After all, who has time to read an entire book every quarter, let alone attend conferences or shadow other leaders? How can we possibly sit down to study new concepts when we're juggling budgets, programs, pastoral care, and personal life responsibilities? Yet the reality is that lifelong learning – investing in our own growth – often creates more time and efficiency down the line.

Here's how to make it work:

1. Prioritize Learning: Block out time weekly for reading, mentorship, or attending workshops. Even 15–30 minutes a day adds up over time.

2. Integrate Learning Into Existing Routines: Use commutes or workouts to listen to audiobooks or podcasts.

3. Build a Learning Community: Form a group with your team or peers to exchange ideas and hold each other accountable.

4. Seek Collaboration: Visit other churches, attend conferences, and seek mentors to gain fresh perspectives.

Conclusion: Learning as a Lifelong Spiritual Discipline

Ultimately, the commitment to never stop learning isn't just a leadership principle—it's a spiritual discipline. The bible repeatedly urges believers to seek wisdom, grow in understanding, and let the mind of Christ transform us day by day (Romans 12:2). By feeding your mind with excellent books, learning from other leaders, and attending conferences or seminars, you position yourself to lead with clarity, innovation, and humility.

Remember, true learning reshapes our hearts and our habits, drawing us closer to the God who created an infinitely complex world. When we model a hunger for growth, we reflect the posture of a disciple—remaining open to the guidance of the Holy Spirit, to new revelations in Scripture, and to the wisdom gleaned from those who have walked this path before us. Never stop learning—it's one of the greatest ways to honor God and equip yourself for greater Kingdom impact.

Reflections Chapter 2: Never Stop Learning—Cultivating a Lifelong Appetite for Growth

Leadership is a dynamic journey, requiring a commitment to lifelong learning. Whether through books, seminars, mentorship, or collaboration with others, the pursuit of knowledge equips us to navigate the complexities of leadership with wisdom and confidence.

Reflection Questions:

1. What areas of leadership do you feel called to learn more about?

2. How can you integrate learning into your daily or weekly schedule?

3. Who can you collaborate with or learn from to expand your perspective?

4. How can you create or participate in a Christ-centered community that fosters accountability and growth?

Chapter 3
Seek Wisdom and Discernment—Choosing the Road Less Traveled

One of the greatest gifts a leader can cultivate is the ability to seek wisdom and discernment. These traits are not innate for most of us—they're developed through intentionality, experience, and most importantly, through a relationship with God. When Solomon became king, he had the humility to recognize that his title alone didn't qualify him to lead. He could have asked God for riches, fame, or power, but instead, he asked for wisdom to govern God's people rightly. In response, God was so pleased that He not only granted Solomon unparalleled wisdom but also blessed him with the wealth and honor he hadn't requested (1 Kings 3:5–14).

This story teaches us that wisdom isn't just about making good decisions; it's about having a heart that seeks to align with God's will. It's about prioritizing what is right in God's eyes over what might be convenient, popular, or politically advantageous. As leaders—whether in the church, the workplace, or our communities—we are constantly faced with choices. Do we seek to please people or God? Do we take shortcuts for personal gain, or do we commit to doing what's right, even when it's hard? The answers to these questions often define the trajectory of our leadership and the legacy we leave behind.

Robert Frost's famous poem, The Road Not Taken, captures this struggle beautifully. Frost reflects on a choice he made between two paths, ultimately deciding to take "the road less traveled by," which made "all the difference." As Christian leaders, we are often called to take that road less traveled—the one that prioritizes integrity over convenience, selflessness over self-promotion, and obedience to God over societal expectations. Walking this road isn't always easy, but it's where we find the joy, peace, and fulfillment that only come from living in alignment with God's purposes. As those already saved by grace, through Christ's sacrifice on our behalf, we don't need to attempt to self-justify!

The Pursuit of Wisdom: God's Perspective vs. Human Wisdom

The Bible consistently contrasts godly wisdom with human wisdom. ***Proverbs 3:5–6*** reminds us to "Trust in the Lord with all your heart and lean not on your own understanding; in all your ways submit to Him, and He will make your paths straight." Human wisdom often relies on logic, personal experience, and cultural norms. While these can be helpful, they are incomplete without the divine perspective. God's wisdom sees beyond the immediate, revealing the eternal consequences of our choices.

In leadership, this distinction is critical. Human wisdom might suggest taking the path that offers the most immediate rewards or the least resistance. Godly wisdom, however, often requires us to make choices that don't make sense to the world but are rooted in obedience to Him , our sovereign God who holds the future in His hands. Solomon's decision to ask for wisdom over wealth or power was countercultural—even today, most leaders prioritize resources or influence over spiritual understanding. Yet Solomon's choice led to blessings far beyond his initial request.

Seeking wisdom also helps us navigate the complexities of leadership, where the "right" choice isn't always obvious. In such moments, discernment becomes indispensable. Discernment is the ability to distinguish between good and best, truth and deception, or God's voice and our own desires. It's what helps us move beyond surface-level decisions and align our actions with God's will.

The Foundation of Wisdom: Prayer, Meditation, and Scripture

The pursuit of wisdom always begins with God. ***James 1:5*** offers this promise: "If any of you lacks wisdom, you should ask God, who gives generously to all without finding fault, and it will be given to you." Prayer is the starting point—our direct line of communication with the Creator of all wisdom. But prayer alone isn't enough. To truly develop wisdom, one must be rooted in a deep study of God's Word, prayer for guidance, and mediation so that God can reveal his truths to us.

When we pray, we acknowledge our dependence on God, asking Him to guide us in our decisions. When we meditate, we create space for

God's wisdom to penetrate our hearts and minds. And when we study Scripture, we arm ourselves with timeless principles that are sufficient (see 2 Tim 3:16-17 and 2Pe 1:3) to help us discern right from wrong, truth from error, and God's will from worldly distractions. Together, these practices form a foundation that not only leads to wise decisions but also transforms us into wise leaders.

Consider the story of Joshua. Before leading the Israelites into the Promised Land, God gave him a critical instruction: "Keep this Book of the Law always on your lips; meditate on it day and night, so that you may be careful to do everything written in it. Then you will be prosperous and successful" *(Joshua 1:8)*. God didn't tell Joshua to rely on military strategies or political alliances. Instead, He pointed Joshua to the importance of staying rooted in His Word. The same principle applies to us today. If we want to lead wisely, we must prioritize God's voice above all others.

Human wisdom might suggest taking the path that offers the most immediate rewards or the least resistance. Godly wisdom, however, often requires us to make choices that don't make sense to the world but are rooted in obedience to Him.

Discernment: Choosing the Right Road

Wisdom helps us see the big picture, but discernment is what helps us choose the right road in specific situations. It's the ability to recognize God's direction, even when it's not the most obvious or comfortable path. As leaders, we face countless decisions: how to handle conflict, where to allocate resources, whom to trust with responsibilities, and how to respond to criticism. Without discernment, we risk making choices based on fear, ego, or external pressures rather than God's guidance.

Discernment – where we must have focused personal effort, aided by the Holy Spirit – often requires us to take a step back and seek clarity through prayer, reflection, and wise counsel. In moments of uncertainty, ask yourself:

- **Does this decision align with God's Word?**

- **Will this choice glorify God or simply serve my own interests?**

- **Am I acting out of faith or fear?**

- **What do trusted, spiritually mature mentors, advisors, or peers say about this?**

These questions help us pause and recalibrate our decision-making process, ensuring that we're not just reacting to circumstances but responding in alignment with God's will.

The Courage to Do What's Right

Wisdom and discernment often lead us to difficult choices. Sometimes, doing the right thing means standing alone. It might mean addressing sin within your team, even if it risks creating tension. It might mean declining a lucrative opportunity that compromises your values. Or it might mean stepping out in faith to pursue a calling that others don't understand.

In such moments, it's tempting to take the easier road—the one that avoids conflict, preserves our comfort, or gains us favor with others. But as Frost's poem reminds us, the road less traveled is often the one that "makes all the difference." For Christians, that difference is eternal. When we choose to do what's right in the eyes of God, we honor Him and create a ripple effect that impacts those around us.

I've seen this principle play out in both ministry and business. In my corporate career, I faced situations where doing the ethical thing wasn't the most profitable option. Yet I found that when I prioritized integrity, God often provided unexpected blessings—sometimes in the form of strengthened relationships, increased trust, or opportunities I couldn't have foreseen. The same holds true in church leadership. When we lead with wisdom and discernment, we create a culture of trust, respect, and spiritual growth.

Practical Steps for Seeking Wisdom and Discernment

1. Commit to Prayer: Make it a habit to pray for wisdom daily. Be specific about the areas where you need guidance, and trust that God will provide clarity.

2. Meditate on Scripture: Regularly reflect on passages that speak to wisdom, such as Proverbs or the teachings of Jesus. Let these truths shape your decision-making process.

3. Seek Counsel: Surround yourself with godly mentors and advisors who can offer perspective and accountability. Proverbs 15:22 reminds us that

"Plans fail for lack of counsel, but with many advisers they succeed."

4. Evaluate Your Motives: Before making a decision, ask yourself why you're leaning toward a particular choice. Are you seeking God's glory or your own comfort?

5. Be Patient: Wisdom often requires waiting for God's timing. Resist the urge to rush decisions out of fear or pressure.

6. Learn from Experience: Reflect on past decisions, both good and bad. What lessons did God teach you through those moments?

The Rewards of Wisdom

When we actively seek wisdom and discernment, the rewards are immeasurable. We gain clarity in our calling, confidence in our decisions, and peace in knowing we're aligned with

God's will. We also inspire those we lead to trust in God's guidance, creating a ripple effect that strengthens the entire community.

Like Solomon, we may find that seeking wisdom brings blessings we never anticipated. These blessings may not always come in material form, but they will undoubtedly include spiritual fruit—greater intimacy with God, deeper relationships with others, and a legacy of faithfulness that outlasts our earthly leadership.

Conclusion: The Road Less Traveled

Leadership is filled with crossroads moments—times when we must choose between the familiar and the faithful, the easy and the ethical, the comfortable and the courageous. Seeking wisdom and discernment ensures that we don't navigate these moments alone. Instead, we invite God to guide us, trusting that His ways are higher than ours.

So take the road less traveled. Prioritize what's right in God's eyes, even when it's unpopular or inconvenient. Build your foundation on prayer, meditation, and Scripture, and let these practices shape your decisions. Surround yourself with wise counselors, and never stop asking God for clarity. As you do, you'll find that the road of wisdom truly does make all the difference—for you, for those you lead, and for the Kingdom of God.

Chapter 3 Reflections: Seek Wisdom and Discernment—Choosing the Right Path

Wisdom and discernment are indispensable for leaders, enabling us to make decisions that honor God and serve His people. By seeking God's guidance through prayer, reflection, and wise counsel, we align our actions with His purposes.

Reflection Questions:

1. What steps do you take to seek God's wisdom in your decisions?

2. How do you distinguish between your own desires and God's will for you and those you are serving?

3. Who are the trusted advisors in your life who help you discern the right path?

Chapter 4
Find Your Blind Spots—Seeing What You Can't See

One of the most difficult, humbling, and transformative lessons in leadership is learning to recognize your blind spots. These are the flaws, habits, or tendencies we cannot see in ourselves but that are obvious to others. Blind spots are dangerous precisely because they're hidden. They can undermine our leadership, damage relationships, and hold us back from reaching our full potential—often without us even realizing it.

What's remarkable is how easy it is for us to spot the blind spots in others. Jesus addressed this tendency in *Matthew 7:3–5*, when He said, "Why do you look at the speck of sawdust in your brother's eye and pay no attention to the plank in your own eye? ... First take the plank out of your own eye, and then you will see clearly to remove the speck from your brother's eye." This passage reminds us that self-awareness is crucial for leadership. If we fail to confront our blind spots, we'll continue to act in ways that hurt ourselves and others—often while criticizing those same flaws in others.

The challenge is that no one likes to have their weaknesses pointed out. It's uncomfortable, sometimes painful, to confront truths about ourselves that we'd rather ignore. But in my experience, whether in business or ministry, the willingness to face and address our blind spots is one of the most impactful things we can do to grow as leaders.

The Hard Lessons from the C-Suite

When I was a C-suite executive, my leadership team implemented an exercise that forced us to confront our blind spots. Once a year, during our quarterly offsite meetings, we dedicated a session to giving each other feedback about our blind spots. Each of us had to share with every other executive something they needed to start doing—or stop doing—for the benefit of the team and the company.

To say this was a tough process is an understatement. We all hated it. No one enjoys being told what they're doing wrong, especially when it comes from peers or colleagues. Yet, it was one of the most impactful exercises we ever did. Why? Because it forced us to confront the things we couldn't see in ourselves. It also forced us to be truth with others that we trusted and respected. These weren't trivial issues, they were behaviors or habits that were actively harming the team, undermining trust, or slowing down progress.

For example, I might not have realized that my communication style came across as dismissive in certain situations or that my tendency to micromanage was frustrating my team. It took someone else pointing it out for me to recognize the pattern and work on changing it, as well as a level of personal humility (and self-control) to embrace and apply this well-meaning input. The same was true for my colleagues. We grew as leaders because we were willing to face these blind spots, painful as they were, and take steps to improve.

The Role of Trust in Revealing Blind Spots

Addressing blind spots is only possible in an environment of trust. You need people around you who are not only willing to tell you the truth but who also have your best interests at heart. In the C-suite, we trusted one another because we shared a common goal: the success of the company. We knew the feedback, however hard to hear, was intended to make us—and the team—better.

In church leadership, this trust is even more critical. Our work isn't just about managing programs or hitting targets; it's about shepherding people and serving God. As leaders, we have to surround ourselves with individuals who love us enough to speak the truth in love (Ephesians 4:15) and who want to see us grow into the leaders God has called us to be.

For me, one of the most trusted voices in my life is my wife. We've been married for over 32 years, and she has a unique ability to see my blind spots and point them out in a way that's honest but loving. She's more of a behind-the-scenes leader, while I tend to be out front, so she offers a perspective I might miss otherwise. There are times when her feedback stings—I don't always like hearing that I got something wrong—but I trust her completely. I know that her words come from a place of love and a desire to help me become a better husband, leader, and servant of God.

As leaders, we have to surround ourselves with individuals who love us enough to speak the truth in love (Ephesians 4:15) and who want to see us grow into the leaders God has called us to be.

The Importance of a Trusted Feedback Circle

If you want to uncover your blind spots, you need to build a trusted feedback circle. These are the people in your life who:

1. Know You Well: They've observed your behavior, habits, and tendencies over time.

2. Care About You: Their feedback comes from a place of love and a desire to see you grow.

3. Are Honest: They're willing to tell you the truth, even when it's uncomfortable.

4. Have Wisdom: Their perspective is grounded in discernment, not just personal opinion.

This feedback circle might include:

- A Mentor: Someone with more experience who can guide you with wisdom and insight.

- A Spouse or Close Friend: Someone who knows you intimately and can offer candid feedback.

- A Trusted Peer: Someone in a similar leadership role who understands the challenges you face.

In ministry, this could also include an elder, deacon, or trusted member of your church who has observed your leadership over time. The key is to choose people who are spiritually mature, emotionally aware, and committed to your growth.

How to Invite Feedback

Creating a culture of honest feedback starts with vulnerability. You have to be willing to admit that you don't have it all together and that you want to grow. Here are some practical steps to invite feedback about your blind spots:

1. Ask Directly: Approach a trusted individual and ask for their honest feedback. For example, "What's one thing you think I could improve on as a leader?" or "In your observation, what is my biggest blind spot?"

2. Be Specific: If you suspect a particular area might be a blind spot, ask about it. For example, "Do you think I communicate clearly during meetings?"

3. Listen Without Defensiveness: Resist the urge to explain or justify your actions. Simply listen and reflect on what they're saying.

4. Thank Them: Express gratitude for their honesty, even if the feedback is hard to hear.

5. Take Action: Use feedback as a starting point for growth. Set specific goals and ask for accountability.

The Role of Mentors in Identifying Blind Spots

A great mentor can be invaluable in helping you uncover blind spots. Mentors bring a level of objectivity and wisdom that's hard to find elsewhere. They've likely walked similar paths and can recognize patterns in your behavior that you might overlook.

In my life, mentors have been instrumental in helping me grow as a leader. They've pointed out areas where I needed to improve, offered practical advice, and encouraged me to pursue excellence. The beauty of a mentor-mentee relationship is that it's built on trust and mutual respect. Your mentor isn't there to tear you down—they're there to help you build a stronger foundation.

Blind Spots in Church Leadership

In church leadership, blind spots can have serious consequences. A lack of self-awareness can lead to poor decision-making, strained relationships, and even spiritual harm to the congregation. Here are a few common blind spots for church leaders:

• **Overcommitment:** Taking on too much and neglecting self-care or family responsibilities.

• **Poor Delegation:** Micromanaging or failing to empower others.

• **Communication Issues:** Not clearly articulating vision or failing to listen to feedback.

- **Ego:** Allowing pride to interfere with collaboration or humility. I've heard this described as when self "edges God out" (i.e., e.g.o.)!

Addressing these blind spots requires humility, prayer, and a willingness to grow. It also requires a commitment to the spiritual disciplines we discussed earlier—prayer, meditation, and Scripture study. These practices keep us grounded in God's truth and help us recognize areas where we need His grace and guidance.

The Impact of Recognizing Blind Spots

When you begin to identify and address your blind spots, you'll notice several positive changes:

1. Improved Relationships: People will respect your willingness to grow and appreciate your efforts to improve.

2. Greater Self-Awareness: You'll start to recognize patterns in your behavior and make adjustments before problems arise.

3. Stronger Leadership: By addressing your weaknesses, you'll become a more effective and trustworthy leader.

4. Spiritual Growth: Confronting your flaws is a humbling process that draws you closer to God and deepens your reliance on Him.

5. Ministry: Others being challenged to address their own blind spots by being inspired through your personal example.

Conclusion: Embrace the Process

Finding your blind spots isn't easy. It requires humility, vulnerability, and a willingness to hear hard truths. But the rewards are worth it. When you invite trusted voices into your life, listen to their feedback, and take steps to grow, you become a stronger, wiser, and more effective leader.

Remember, we all have blind spots. The goal isn't perfection—it's progress. As you continue to seek wisdom, surround yourself with godly counsel, and walk in humility, you'll reflect more of Christ in your leadership. And that, ultimately, is what matters most.

Chapter 4 Reflections: Find Your Blind Spots—Seeing What You Can't See

Every leader has blind spots—areas of weakness or unawareness that can hinder their effectiveness. Recognizing and addressing these blind spots requires vulnerability, humility, and input from trusted voices.

Reflection Questions:

1. Who in your life can you trust to point out your blind spots?

2. How do you typically respond to constructive feedback?

3. What changes can you make to create an environment where honest feedback is welcomed?

Chapter 5
Find Your Passion and What You're Really Good At—Aligning Your Gifts with God's Calling

One of the most important steps in becoming an effective leader in the church is identifying your passion and your strengths. Christ-centered passion fuels your energy and commitment, while your strengths—what you're truly good at—enable you to serve effectively and make a meaningful impact. While these two things often overlap, they aren't always the same. Recognizing the distinction and aligning both with your spiritual leadership can lead to a more fulfilling and fruitful journey.

In this chapter, we'll explore how to identify your passion, uncover your strengths, and bring these elements together to serve in a way that glorifies God and maximizes your potential.

The Importance of Passion in Leadership

Passion is the fire that drives us. It's the thing that excites you, motivates you, and keeps you going even when the work is hard or the challenges seem insurmountable. Christ-centered passion is what allows leaders to pour their hearts into their work, inspiring others and staying resilient in the face of adversity.

A. W. Tozer, renowned for his Christian classics "The Pursuit of God" and "The Knowledge of the Holy," encouraged all of us to be passionate about seeking God. Additionally, Tozer stated that we should, "Refuse to be average. Let your heart soar as high as it will," encouraging individuals to earnestly pursue their spiritual journey without settling for mediocrity. I believe that when you discover what you truly care about, work no longer feels like a burden—it becomes a joy.

In the context of church leadership, passion takes on an even deeper dimension. It's not just about finding something you enjoy; it's about discovering the intersection between what you love and what God is calling you to do. He has divinely placed us in our role, place, and time for His purposes. Passion in ministry often reflects the unique burdens God places on our hearts—whether it's a passion for teaching, evangelism, music, youth ministry, or social justice. When you serve in an area that aligns with your passion, your work not only becomes more meaningful but also more effective.

For example, if you're passionate about helping the homeless, you might feel a deep sense of purpose leading your church's outreach ministry. If you love teaching and inspiring others, you might thrive as a Bible study leader or Sunday School teacher. Passion gives you the energy to persist in your calling, even when the demands are great.

Discovering Your Passion

As you consider serving in a leadership role in the church, it's essential to reflect on the things you're truly passionate about. Here are a few steps to help you uncover your passion:

1. Reflect on What Moves You: Think about the moments in church or ministry when you've felt most alive and fulfilled. Was it during a worship service? A mission trip? Teaching a class? These moments often point to the areas where your passion lies.

2. Ask Questions: Take time to ask yourself questions like:

o   What breaks my heart or stirs my soul when I see a need in the world?

o   What excites me when I think about serving in the church?

o Where do I feel God's presence most strongly when I serve?

3. Look for Patterns: Passion often reveals itself through recurring themes in your life. For instance, if you've always found joy in mentoring others, you might be passionate about discipleship or leadership development.

4. Pray for Clarity: Ask God to reveal the desires He's placed in your heart and to guide you toward the areas where He wants you to serve.

Passion isn't always immediately obvious. Sometimes, it takes time and exploration to uncover what truly excites and energizes you. If you're unsure, start by serving in different roles and pay attention to how each one resonates with you. As you step out in faith, God will often confirm your passions through the joy and fulfillment you experience.

The Role of Strengths in Leadership

While passion fuels your work, your strengths determine how effectively you can carry it out. Strengths are the natural talents, skills, and abilities God has given you. We *all* have many God-given gifts (e.g., 1 Cor 12:1-11, Ro 12:6-8, 1Pe 4:10-11). They're the things you excel at, often without even realizing it, because they come so naturally.

It's important to recognize that passion and strengths don't always align perfectly. You might be passionate about singing but not have a strong singing voice. Conversely, you might be an excellent organizer but not feel passionate about event planning. However, when you can bring your strengths into an area you're passionate about, you create a powerful synergy that amplifies your impact.

For example, I've always loved teaching and motivating others. It's one of the main reasons I'm writing this book. I want to push you to become a better leader and to move into greater roles of influence within the church. Teaching and inspiring others is not only something I'm passionate about, but it's also something I've developed as a strength through years of experience in ministry and business leadership.

Uncovering Your Strengths

Identifying your strengths requires self-reflection, feedback from others, and a willingness to acknowledge both your gifts and your limitations. Here are some practical ways to discover your strengths:

1. Reflect on Your Past Successes: Think about the times when you've excelled in a role, project, or task. What skills or qualities contributed to your

success? For example, were you particularly good at communicating, organizing, problem-solving, or leading a team?

2. Seek Feedback: Ask trusted family members, friends, or colleagues to share what they see as your greatest strengths. Sometimes, others can see qualities in us that we overlook.

3. Take Assessments: Tools like StrengthsFinder, spiritual gifts inventories, or personality assessments can provide valuable insights into your natural abilities and how they might align with leadership roles in the church.

4. Experiment and Evaluate: Try serving in different roles and pay attention to where you feel most effective and confident. Your strengths often become more apparent when you're actively using them.

Aligning Passion and Strengths with Your Calling

The ultimate goal is to bring your passion and strengths into alignment with God's calling on your life. This doesn't mean you'll always serve in areas where you're both passionate and highly skilled. Sometimes God calls us to step out of our comfort zones and develop new skills. Other times, He uses us in areas where we're passionate but may need additional support from others who complement our weaknesses.

However, when you can find roles that align with both your passion and your strengths, your work becomes more impactful and sustainable. For example:

• If you're passionate about teaching and also a gifted communicator, you might thrive as a Bible study leader or Sunday School teacher.

- If you're passionate about social justice and skilled in organization, you might excel in leading a community outreach program.

- If you're passionate about worship and gifted in music, you might find fulfillment in serving on the worship team.

A Practical Exercise for Self-Discovery

I want to challenge you to spend time this week reflecting on your passion and strengths. Here's a simple exercise to guide you:

1. Set Aside 30 Minutes for Reflection: Find a quiet space and write down your answers to the following questions:

o What am I most passionate about in church or ministry?

o What are the activities that bring me the greatest joy and fulfillment (especially when I sense God's pleasure)?

o What are the skills or talents that come naturally to me?

2. Spend 30 Minutes with a Trusted Friend or Family Member: Ask them to share what they see as your greatest strengths and gifts. You might be surprised by their insights. Sometimes others can see potential in us that we overlook.

3. Pray for Guidance: Ask God to reveal how your passion and strengths can be used for His glory. Surrender your plans to Him and trust that He will guide you to the right opportunities.

Embrace Your Unique Role in the Body of Christ

The beauty of the church is that it functions as a body, with each member playing a unique role. *1 Corinthians 12:4–7* reminds us, "There are different kinds of gifts, but the same Spirit distributes them. There are different kinds of service, but the same Lord. There are different kinds of working, but in all of them and in everyone it is the same God at work." Your passion and strengths are part of God's design for the church. When you operate in alignment with your gifts, you contribute to the health and growth of the body.

TAKE TIME TO DISCOVER YOUR PASSION AND TALENTS

Conclusion: Start Where You Are

Discovering your passion and strengths isn't a one-time event; it's an ongoing process of self-discovery and surrender. As you explore new roles and seek God's guidance, you'll gain greater clarity about how He has uniquely equipped you to serve.

Remember, your leadership journey doesn't have to be perfect, it just has to be faithful. Take the first step by reflecting on what excites you and where you excel. Seek feedback from those who know you best, and trust God to reveal the path ahead. When you lead with passion and strength, fueled by God's calling, you'll find joy and fulfillment that transcends the challenges of leadership. Let this be the season where you fully embrace who God created you to be, for His glory and the good of His church.

Chapter 5 Reflections: Find Your Passion and What You're Really Good At—Aligning Gifts with Calling

Passion fuels your energy and commitment, while strength enables you to serve effectively. By discovering and aligning these elements with God's calling, you can lead with purpose and joy.

Reflection Questions:

1. What activities or roles in the church bring you the most joy?

2. What talents or skills come naturally to you that could be used for God's glory?

3. Have you asked trusted family or friends to identify your strengths? What did you learn?

Chapter 6
Stretch Beyond Where You Are— Breaking Through Fear and Doubt

One of the greatest challenges—and opportunities—for any leader is learning to stretch beyond where you are. Growth as a leader often requires stepping into roles or responsibilities that make you uncomfortable, demand new skills, or push you to confront your fears. These moments are not easy, but they are essential. They allow us to grow in confidence, reliance on God, and our ability to serve others.

As Christians, we know that fear and doubt are two of Satan's most effective weapons. They whisper to us that we're not good enough, smart enough, or capable enough to succeed. But Scripture reminds us otherwise. ***Philippians 4:13*** boldly declares, "I can do all things through Christ who strengthens me." This verse doesn't promise that every challenge will be easy or that success will come instantly, but it does promise that God's strength is sufficient for whatever He calls us to do. Our gracious, merciful and loving God will always provide us with everything we need to accomplish what He is truly asking of us! When we embrace this truth, we can stretch beyond our current abilities, trusting that God will equip us for the work He has set before us.

Fear and Doubt: Satan's Tools to Keep You Stuck

Fear and doubt are universal human experiences, but they become especially potent when we step into leadership. The fear of failure, criticism, or inadequacy can paralyze even the most capable leader. Doubt, meanwhile, undermines our confidence and convinces us to play small, avoiding risks that might lead to growth.

As leaders, we must recognize fear and doubt for what they are: tools of the enemy designed to keep us from fulfilling God's purpose. *2 Timothy 1:7* reminds us, "For God has not given us a spirit of fear, but of power and of love and of a sound mind." When we allow fear and doubt to dictate our decisions, we're essentially saying that we don't trust God to sustain us. But when we step out in faith, even in the face of uncertainty, we declare our trust in His power and provision.

Learning to Stretch: A Personal Example

For me, one area where I've had to stretch is in leading hymns during our Sunday School opening. As the Sunday School Superintendent, I'm responsible for leading the congregation in two hymns every Sunday morning. Here's the obvious truth: I'm not a great singer. In fact, singing in front of others pushes me far outside my comfort zone. But I do it because it's part of my role, and I believe it's important to set an example for others.

By stepping up to lead these hymns, even though it's not my strength, I hope to show others that it's okay to serve in areas where they might feel uncomfortable. If they see me, someone who isn't naturally gifted in singing, leading hymns with enthusiasm, they might think, "If he can do that, I can do this." My goal isn't to impress anyone with my voice—it's to inspire them to stretch beyond their own comfort zones and step into roles where God can use them.

Stretching beyond where you are doesn't always look glamorous. Sometimes it's as simple as volunteering to help in a ministry where you don't feel particularly confident or skilled. Other times, it might mean taking on a leadership role you've never held before. Whatever the situation, the process of stretching challenges us to rely less on our own abilities and more on God's strength.

The Growth That Comes from Stretching

When you stretch beyond your current abilities, you grow in several keyways:

1. You Build Confidence: Each time you step outside your comfort zone and succeed—no matter how small the success—you gain confidence. That confidence isn't rooted in arrogance but in the realization that God truly equips those He calls.

2. You Overcome Fear: Fear loses its power when you face it head-on. The more you step into challenging situations, the more you realize that fear is often just a barrier we build in our own minds.

3. You Inspire Others: As a leader, your willingness to stretch beyond your comfort zone sets an example for those around you. It encourages them to do the same, creating a culture of growth and faith within your church or ministry.

4. You Discover Hidden Strengths: Often, we don't know what we're capable of until we're pushed to try something new. By stretching beyond your current role or skill set, you may discover talents or abilities you didn't know you had.

5. You Strengthen Your Faith: When you step into areas where you feel inadequate, you're forced to rely on God in a deeper way. That dependence on Him strengthens your faith and deepens your relationship with Him.

Practical Ways to Stretch Beyond Where You Are

Stretching beyond where you are doesn't have to be a dramatic leap. It can begin with small, intentional steps. Here are some practical ways to start stretching in your leadership:

1. Serve in an Unfamiliar Role: Look for areas in your church where help is needed, even if it's not a role you'd naturally gravitate toward. For example, if you've always worked in administrative roles, consider volunteering in youth ministry or outreach. You might surprise yourself with how much you enjoy it.

2. Say Yes to Opportunities: When your pastor or another leader asks for help in a new area, don't immediately dismiss it because it's outside your comfort zone. Consider it an opportunity to grow and serve in a new way.

3. Set Personal Goals: Identify one area where you'd like to grow as a leader and set a specific goal to stretch yourself in that area. For example, if public speaking makes you nervous, volunteer to give a short devotion or lead a prayer during a church meeting.

4. Invite Feedback: Ask trusted mentors or colleagues where they think you could stretch or grow as a leader. Their insights might reveal opportunities you hadn't considered.

5. Pray for Boldness: Ask God to give you the courage to step into new roles or responsibilities. Remember, He equips those He calls.

Encouraging Others to Stretch

As a leader, part of your role is to encourage others to stretch beyond where they are. Here are some ways to inspire growth in those you lead:

1. Lead by Example: Your willingness to stretch sets the tone for your team or congregation. When others see you stepping into uncomfortable roles or trying new things, they'll be more likely to do the same.

2. Offer Opportunities: Look for ways to challenge others by giving them new responsibilities or inviting them to serve in different roles. For example, if someone in your church has a gift for hospitality, encourage them to lead an event or coordinate a ministry.

3. Provide Support: Stretching can be intimidating, so make sure those you're challenging feel supported. Offer guidance, encouragement, and resources to help them succeed.

4. Celebrate Growth: When someone steps out of their comfort zone and grows as a result, acknowledge and celebrate their progress. This reinforces the value of stretching and encourages others to follow suit.

Confronting Fear and Doubt

Stretching beyond where you are often requires confronting fear and doubt head-on. These emotions are natural, but they don't have to control you. Here are some practical ways to overcome fear and doubt as you step into new roles:

1. Claim God's Promises: Memorize and meditate on verses like Philippians 4:13 and 2 Timothy 1:7. These truths remind us that God's power is greater than our fears.

2. Focus on Growth, Not Perfection: Remember that stretching is about progress, not perfection. It's okay to make mistakes as long as you're learning and growing.

3. Take Small Steps: Start with manageable challenges and gradually work your way up to bigger ones. Each small success builds momentum for the next step.

4. Pray for Strength: Ask God to give you the courage and wisdom to face new challenges. Prayer not only strengthens your faith but also aligns your heart with God's will.

Conclusion: A Life of Growth and Faith

Stretching beyond where you are isn't just about personal growth—it's about fulfilling God's purpose for your life. When you step into roles or responsibilities that challenge you, you're not only growing as a leader but also glorifying God by trusting Him to equip you.

As you continue to lead, remember that fear and doubt are natural, but they don't have to define you. Through Christ, you have the strength to do more than you ever thought possible. So take that first step. Stretch beyond your current abilities, trust God to guide you, and watch as He uses you in ways you never imagined. By doing so, you'll inspire others to do the same, creating a ripple effect of faith and growth in your church and community.

Chapter 6 Reflections: Stretch Beyond Where You Are—Overcoming Fear and Doubt

Growth as a leader often requires stepping into roles or responsibilities that make you uncomfortable. By confronting fear and doubt and trusting in God's strength, you can stretch beyond your current abilities and discover new potential.

Reflection Questions:

1. What opportunities have you avoided because they felt outside your comfort zone?

2. How can you rely on God's strength to face challenges with confidence?

3. What example can you set for others by stepping into unfamiliar roles?

Chapter 7
Learn to Walk in Love—The Greatest Commandment for Leadership

If there's one principle that can elevate your leadership to extraordinary levels, it is learning to walk in the love of Christ. Love is not just an emotion or sentiment; it is a conscious decision to act with kindness, patience, truth and grace—even when it's difficult. In ministry, in business, and in life, walking in love is a hallmark of true leadership. When Jesus was asked to identify the greatest commandment, He gave a profound yet simple answer: "Love the Lord your God with all your heart and with all your soul and with all your mind. This is the first and greatest commandment. And the second is like it: Love your neighbor as yourself" ***(Matthew 22:37–39)***. These two commandments encapsulate the heart of leadership, ministry, and the Christian life. He also said that His followers are to "Love one another, just as I have loved you" and "They will know us by our love" (Jn 13:34-35).

Yet, walking in love isn't always easy. People aren't perfect. They make mistakes, they frustrate us, and sometimes they even work against us. The devil is constantly at work, using misunderstandings, conflicts, and offenses to derail our leadership and sow division. But as leaders, we are called to rise above these challenges by embodying Christ's love in our words, actions, and attitudes. When we do, we not only honor God but also create an environment where others can thrive, grow, and experience His grace.

The Foundation of Love in Leadership

Walking in love begins with understanding the centrality of love in the Christian life. *1 Corinthians 13*, often referred to as the "love chapter," provides a beautiful and practical description of what love looks like in action. Paul writes:

"Love is patient, love is kind. It does not envy, it does not boast, it is not proud. It does not dishonor others, it is not self-seeking, it is not easily angered, it keeps no record of wrongs. Love does not delight in evil but rejoices with the truth. It always protects, always trusts, always hopes, always perseveres. Love never fails" (1 Corinthians 13:4–8).

These verses remind us that love is not merely a feeling, it is a set of deliberate choices and behaviors. As leaders, we must choose patience when others test our limits, kindness when others seem undeserving, and forgiveness when we've been wronged. These choices aren't easy, but they are essential if we want to reflect Christ's character in our leadership.

LEARNING TO WALK IN GOD'S LOVE

Love as the Foundation of Jesus' Ministry

Jesus Himself modeled this kind of love throughout His ministry. He loved the unlovable, forgave the unforgivable, and served with humility and compassion. Consider His interaction with the woman caught in adultery *(John 8:1–11)*. While others were ready to condemn her, Jesus responded with grace and love, challenging her accusers and giving her an opportunity to change her life. His gracious love didn't ignore sin, but it sought restoration rather than punishment.

As leaders, we are called to follow this example. Love doesn't mean we avoid difficult conversations, embrace untruths, or ignore problems, but it does mean that our actions and decisions are motivated by a desire to build up rather than tear down. When we lead with love, we create a culture of grace, trust, and mutual respect—

qualities that are essential for any successful team or ministry.

Overcoming Challenges to Walking in Love

Walking in love sounds simple, but in practice, it's anything but. The devil is always looking for opportunities to frustrate us, sow division, and derail our efforts. As leaders, we must be vigilant against these tactics and commit to responding in love, even in challenging situations.

1. Dealing with Difficult People

Every leader encounters difficult people—those who are critical, uncooperative, or disruptive. It's easy to become frustrated or defensive, but love calls us to a higher standard. *Ephesians 4:2* encourages us to "Be completely humble and gentle; be patient, bearing with one another in love." This doesn't mean we ignore issues or enable bad behavior, but it does mean that we address conflicts with humility, seeking resolution rather than revenge.

2. Handling Criticism

Criticism can sting, especially when it feels unfair or personal. Yet, walking in love requires us to respond with grace rather than retaliation. Take a moment to pray, reflect, and seek God's wisdom before responding. Ask yourself: "Is there truth in this criticism? How can I grow from it?" By responding in love, you not only diffuse tension but also model humility and maturity for others.

3. Forgiving Offenses

Forgiveness is one of the hardest aspects of walking in love, but it is also one of the most important. Unforgiveness weighs us down and hinders our ability to lead effectively. ***Colossians 3:13*** reminds us to "Forgive as the Lord forgave you." When we choose to forgive, we model a small portion of the grace God has extended to us (Col 3:13-14), releasing the burden of resentment, and we create space for healing and reconciliation.

4. Balancing Love and Boundaries

Walking in love doesn't mean allowing others to take advantage of you or ignoring unhealthy behavior. It's important to set boundaries that protect your time, energy, and emotional well-being. Love sometimes means saying no, offering constructive feedback, or holding others accountable—all while maintaining an attitude of respect and grace.

The Transformational Power of Love in Leadership

When you learn to walk in love, it transforms not only your leadership but also the lives of those you lead. Here are some of the ways love elevates your leadership:

1. It Builds Trust: Love creates a foundation of trust, which is essential for effective leadership. When people know that you genuinely care about them, they are more likely to follow your guidance and support your vision.

2. It Inspires Others: Love is contagious. When you lead with love, you inspire others to do the same. Your example encourages your team to treat each other with kindness, respect, and compassion, creating a positive and collaborative environment.

3. It Reflects Christ: Ultimately, walking in love reflects the character of Christ and draws others to Him. When people see Christ's love in your leadership, they are more likely to be open to His message and His work in their lives.

4. It Breaks Down Barriers: Love has the power to overcome divisions, heal wounds, and bring people together. In a world often marked by conflict and division, a leader who walks in love stands out as a beacon of hope and unity.

Love is contagious. When you lead with love, you inspire others to do the same.

Also, when you learn to walk in love, it transforms not only your leadership but also the lives of those you lead.

Practical Steps to Walk in Love

Walking in love is a daily commitment that requires intentionality and effort. Here are some practical steps to help you lead with love:

1. Start with Prayer: Begin each day by asking God to fill your heart with His love and to help you see others through His eyes. Pray for the wisdom to respond with grace in challenging situations.

2. Practice Patience: When frustrations arise, take a deep breath and remind yourself to be patient. Reflect on how God has been patient with you and extend that same grace to others.

3. Focus on Encouragement: Look for opportunities to build others up with your words and actions. A kind word or a small act of kindness can have a powerful impact.

4. Be Quick to Forgive: Don't let offenses linger. Choose forgiveness, even when it's hard, and trust God to handle the rest.

5. Lead by Example: Model love in your interactions, even when it's difficult. Your example will inspire others to follow suit.

6. Meditate on Scripture: Regularly reflect on passages about love, such as 1 Corinthians 13, Matthew 22:37–39, and Colossians 3:12–14. Let these verses guide your thoughts and actions.

A Higher Calling

As leaders, we are called to a higher standard. Walking in love is not optional—it is central to our faith and our leadership. When we lead with love, we reflect the heart of Christ, build stronger relationships, and create a lasting impact. It's not always easy, but it is always worth it.

So, as you continue your journey of leadership, remember the words of Jesus: "Love the Lord your God with all your heart and with all your soul and with all your mind … and love your neighbor as yourself" (Matthew 22:37–39). Let these commandments guide your actions and watch as God uses your love to transform lives, strengthen your ministry, and glorify His name. When you learn to walk in love, your leadership will truly reach another level.

Chapter 7 Reflections: Learn to Walk in Love—The Greatest Commandment for Leadership

Love is the foundation of Christian leadership. When we lead with love and unity, we reflect Christ's character, build trust, and create an environment where others can thrive. Walking in love is not always easy, but it is always worth it.

Reflection Questions:

1. How do you currently demonstrate love in your leadership?

2. What challenges make it difficult for you to lead with love, and how can you overcome them?

3. How can you reflect Christ's love to those who frustrate or challenge you?

Conclusion
Transforming Leadership Through Faith, Wisdom, and Love

Leadership is not just a role—it's a calling. Whether in the church, the workplace, or the community, effective leadership requires more than just position, skills or strategies. It demands a heart that is aligned with God's purposes, a willingness to grow, and a commitment to serve others with humility and love. Over the course of this journey, we've explored seven foundational traits that can transform your leadership: prayer, meditation, and Scripture study; a commitment to lifelong learning; the pursuit of wisdom and discernment; recognizing and addressing blind spots; discovering your passion and strengths; stretching beyond your comfort zone; and, above all, walking in love.

Each of these principles is vital on its own, but when woven together, they create a holistic approach to leadership that is grounded in faith, resilience, and grace. Let's reflect on how these traits come together to shape a leader who is equipped to glorify God, inspire others, and make a lasting impact.

Leadership Begins with a Strong Spiritual Foundation

At the heart of transformative leadership is a deep, personal connection with God. This connection is nurtured through **prayer, meditation, and Scripture study.** These disciplines are the foundation upon which all other aspects of leadership are built. Prayer aligns our hearts with God's will, meditation allows us to hear His voice in the stillness, and Scripture provides the unchanging truth that guides our decisions.

Without this foundation, leadership becomes a matter of human effort, prone to burnout and misdirection. But when we root our leadership in God's presence, we gain clarity, strength, and purpose. This spiritual grounding not only equips us to lead effectively but also transforms us from the inside out, enabling us to reflect Christ's character in all that we do. It also gives our leadership eternal impact.

The Journey of Growth: Lifelong Learning and Stretching

Leadership is a dynamic journey, not a static position. It requires a commitment to **lifelong learning** and a willingness to **stretch beyond where you are**. Growth happens when we step outside our comfort zones, embrace new challenges, and remain open to learning from others. Whether it's reading books, attending seminars, or seeking out mentors/wise counsel, the pursuit of knowledge equips us with the tools and perspectives needed to navigate the complexities of leadership.

Stepping into unfamiliar roles or responsibilities can be daunting, but it is in these moments that we grow the most. When we stretch beyond what we think we can handle, we discover new strengths and deepen our reliance on God. This willingness to learn and grow not only enhances our leadership but also inspires others to do the same, creating a culture of growth and resilience within our teams and communities.

Self-Awareness and the Role of Others

No leader is perfect. We all have **blind spots**—flaws or tendencies we can't see in ourselves but that are obvious to others. Recognizing and addressing these blind spots is one of the most humbling and transformative aspects of leadership. It requires vulnerability, a willingness to receive feedback, and the courage to make changes.

Trusted voices, such as mentors, colleagues, or loved ones, play a critical role in helping us see what we cannot. They provide the perspective and accountability we need to grow. For me, my wife has been one of the most important people in this regard, offering honest feedback that, while sometimes uncomfortable, has made me a better leader and person. Surrounding yourself with people who care about your growth and are willing to speak the truth in love is essential for long-term success.

Passion, Strengths, and Calling

Leadership flourishes when we align our **passion** and **strengths** with God's calling. Passion fuels our commitment and energy, while strengths enable us to serve effectively. However, as we've explored, these two elements are not always the same. Discovering what excites you and where your natural abilities lie requires reflection, feedback, and prayer.

When you bring your passion and strengths together in service to God, your work becomes more than just a task—it becomes a ministry. Whether you're teaching, leading worship, organizing events, or serving in outreach, operating in alignment with your God-given gifts allows you to serve with joy, purpose, and impact. Moreover, encouraging others to identify and use their own gifts strengthens the entire body of Christ, fulfilling the vision of 1 Corinthians 12, where every member of the church plays a unique and valuable role.

The Courage to Lead with Love

At the core of everything is **love**. Love is the foundation of Christ's teachings and the defining characteristic of Christian leadership. It's what enables us to lead with grace, build trust, and inspire others. Love is patient and kind, even when others test our limits. It forgives offenses and seeks reconciliation. It prioritizes relationships over results, valuing people not for what they can do but for who they are.

Walking in love is not easy. It requires humility, selflessness, and a commitment to God's greatest commandments: to love Him with all our heart, soul, and mind, and to love our neighbors as ourselves. But when we lead with love, we reflect Christ to those we serve, creating an environment where people feel valued, supported, and empowered to grow.

Facing Challenges with Faith and Resilience

Leadership is not without its challenges. Fear, doubt, criticism, and conflict are inevitable in this fallen world. But as we've seen throughout this journey, these challenges are also opportunities for growth. By grounding ourselves in prayer, seeking wisdom, addressing blind spots, and stepping out in faith, we can overcome the obstacles that come our way.

It's important to remember that leadership is not about perfection—it's about faithfulness. It's about showing up, staying committed, and trusting God to work through our weaknesses. As Paul writes in ***2 Corinthians 12:9***, "My grace is sufficient for you, for my power is made perfect in weakness." When we rely on God's strength rather than our own, we can face any challenge with confidence and resilience.

The Ripple Effect of Godly Leadership

When you embody these seven traits, your leadership has a ripple effect that extends far beyond your immediate context, multiplying even into eternity. Your example inspires others to grow, serve, and lead with integrity. Your decisions, guided by wisdom and love, create a positive and lasting impact on those around you. And most importantly, your leadership glorifies God, pointing others to Him as the ultimate source of hope, purpose, and strength.

As you lead, remember that your influence is not limited to your title or position. Leadership is about stewardship—faithfully using the gifts, opportunities, and relationships God has entrusted to you to further His kingdom. Whether you're leading a church, a team, or your family, you have the power to make a difference by leading with faith, wisdom, and love.

A Final Call to Action

As we conclude this journey, I want to challenge you to take the next step in your leadership. Reflect on the seven traits we've discussed and ask yourself:

1. Am I rooted in Scripture, prayer, and meditation?

2. Am I committed to lifelong learning?

3, Am I seeking wisdom and discernment?

4. Have I invited others to help me see and address my blind spots?

5. Am I serving in alignment with my passion and strengths?

6. Am I stretching beyond my comfort zone?

7. Am I leading with love, even in difficult situations?

Take time this week to pray, reflect, and seek God's guidance. Ask Him to reveal the areas where He wants you to grow and to give you the courage to take the necessary steps. Consider sharing this journey with a trusted friend, mentor, or small group, inviting them to hold you accountable and encourage you along the way.

The Legacy of Leadership

Leadership is not about achieving perfection or acclaim—it's about making a difference for God's glory. When you lead with faith, wisdom, and love, you leave a legacy that honors Him and impacts others for generations to come. My prayer for you is that as you embrace these principles, you will grow into the Christ-centric leader God created you to be, experiencing the joy, fulfillment, and purpose that come from serving Him wholeheartedly.

Remember, you can do all things through Christ who strengthens you. So step out in faith, lead with courage, and let God use you to transform lives and build His kingdom. The journey won't always be easy, but it will always be worth it. May your leadership shine as a reflection of His love, grace, and glory.

Conclusion: Transforming Leadership Through Faith, Wisdom, and Love

Leadership is a journey of growth, service, and transformation. By embodying these seven principles, you can become the leader God created you to be, making a lasting impact for His Kingdom. My prayer is that this book will inspire you to lead with courage, humility, and love, trusting in God to guide you every step of the way.

Acknowledgments

Thank those who have supported and inspired you throughout your leadership journey, starting with our purposeful Creator, Savior, and Sustainer and including mentors, colleagues, and loved ones.

About the Author

John K. Lomax is a devoted church leader at Turner's Chapel AME Church in High Point, North Carolina, where he currently serves as Steward Pro Tem, Sunday School Superintendent, and Senior Class Leader. After spending five years in Birmingham, Alabama, as the Chief Operations Officer at Summer Classics, he is thrilled to be back home in North Carolina, continuing his ministry and leadership work.

John's passion lies in helping leaders realize their full potential. He believes that while a few leaders, like Apostle Paul and King David, are born, most leaders are made over time through growth and perseverance—just like Peter, Timothy, and John Mark. Through this book, he hopes to inspire leaders to embrace these seven principles, helping all of us become better stewards of God's calling and more effective in our service to His Kingdom.

Visit my website for more books, resources, and updates!

Scan to connect with the author or explore more content.

Want more? Scan here to stay inspired and informed.

Go to Amazon to leave a review

Go to Website

www.ingramcontent.com/pod-product-compliance
Lightning Source LLC
LaVergne TN
LVHW021826060526
838201LV00058B/3520